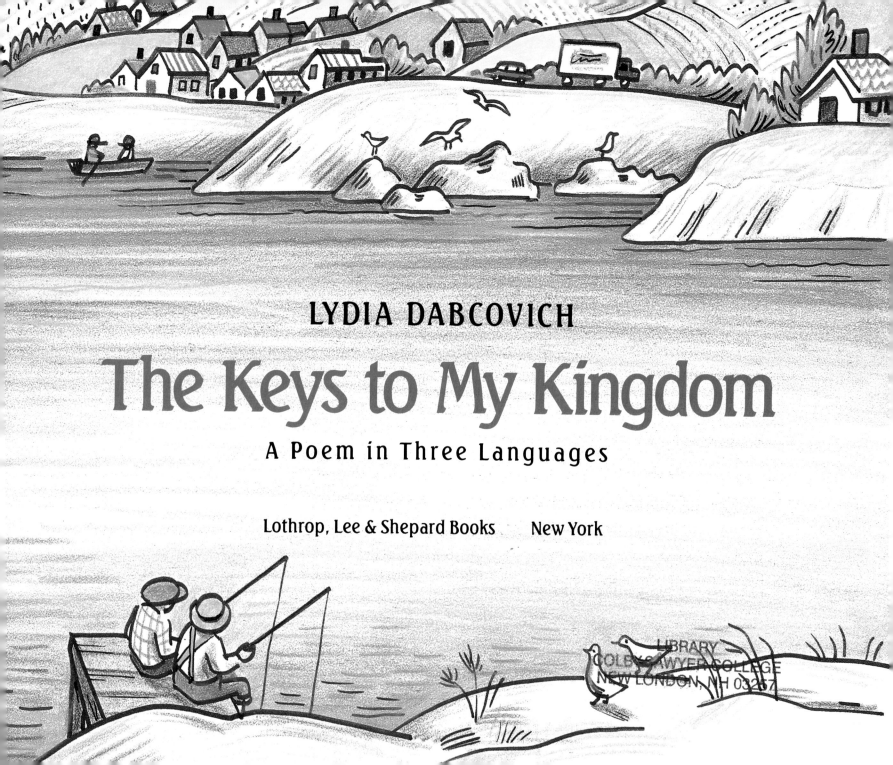

LYDIA DABCOVICH

The Keys to My Kingdom

A Poem in Three Languages

Lothrop, Lee & Shepard Books   New York

Spanish translation by Ana M. Cerro.
With thanks to Laurie Sale, Didi Charney, and Michel Sasson
for their help with the translations.

First Edition 1 2 3 4 5 6 7 8 9 10

Library of Congress Cataloging in Publication Data
Dabcovich, Lydia. The keys to my kingdom : a poem in three languages / by Lydia Dabcovich.
p.   cm.   Summary: Retells the traditional nursery rhyme which takes the reader through the kingdom
and through the day.   ISBN 0-688-09774-X.—ISBN 0-688-09775-8 (lib. bdg.)   I. Nursery rhymes.
2. Children's poetry.   [I. Nursery rhymes.]   I. Title. PZ8.3.D132Ke   1992   398.8—dc20
90-40402   CIP   AC

These are the keys to my kingdom.

Voici les clefs de mon royaume.

Estas son las llaves de mi reino.

In that kingdom there is a city;

Dans ce royaume il y a une ville;

En ese reino hay una ciudad;

In that city there is a town;

Dans cette ville il y a un bourg;

En esa ciudad hay una vecindad;

In that town there is a street;

Dans ce bourg il y a une rue;

En esa vecindad hay una calle;

In that street there is a lane;

Dans cette rue il y a une allée;

En esa calle hay un camino;

In that lane there is a yard;

Dans cette allée il y a une cour;

En ese camino hay un patio;

In that yard there is a house;

Dans cette cour il y a une maison;

En ese patio hay una casa;

In that house there is a room;

Dans cette maison il y a une chambre;

En esa casa hay un cuarto;

In that room there is a bed;

Dans cette chambre il y a un lit;

En ese cuarto hay una cama;

On that bed there is a basket;

Sur ce lit il y a une corbeille;

Sobre esa cama hay una cesta;

In that basket there are some flowers.

Dans cette corbeille il y a des fleurs.

En esa cesta hay unas flores.

Flowers in the basket—

Les fleurs dans la corbeille—

Las flores en la cesta—

Basket on the bed; bed in the room; room in the house;

La corbeille sur le lit; le lit dans la chambre; la chambre dans la maison;

La cesta sobre la cama; la cama en el cuarto; el cuarto en la casa;

House in the yard; yard in the lane; lane in the street;

La maison dans la cour; la cour dans l'allée; l'allée dans la rue;

La casa en el patio; el patio en el camino; el camino en la calle;

Street in the town; town in the city; city in the kingdom;

La rue dans le bourg; le bourg dans la ville; la ville dans le royaume;

La calle en la vecindad; la vecindad en la ciudad; la ciudad en el reino;

And here are the keys to my kingdom;

Et ici se trouvent les clefs de mon royaume;

Y aquí están las llaves de mi reino;

Of my kingdom these are the keys.

Les clefs de mon royaume, les voici.

Las llaves de mi reino, éstas son.